This book belongs to

_____

_____

_____

_____

FLY ANGLER'S LOG

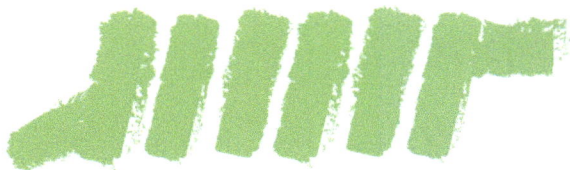

THE FISHING OBSERVATIONS OF:

_____

Anglers gather observations and lessons
from each trip to the river.
Every refusal of a fly or hookup
with a monster tells a story.

Gathering those stories develops
experience and expertise, but most of all,
it builds a life shaped by fly fishing.

Our memories can be lost to time,
but what we record in these pages
passes our life lessons along
to anyone who reads them.

Keep mending.

"Each step into a river presents the opportunity
to discover a truth not apparent before."
Scott Lowe

TRIP LOG

Page	Date & Location
6	
8	
10	
12	
14	
16	
18	
20	
22	
24	
26	
28	
30	
32	
34	
36	
38	
40	
42	
44	
46	
48	
50	
52	
54	

TRIP LOG

Page	Date & Location
56	
58	
60	
62	
64	
66	
68	
70	
72	
74	
76	
78	
80	
82	
84	
86	
88	
90	
92	
94	
96	
98	
100	
102	
104	

F I S H L O G

Date:	Species	Size	Fly	Rig	Lie	Time
Duration: Begin: End:						
Stream:						
Location/Access:						
Weather:						
Temperature: Air: Water:						
Discharge/Stage:						
Companions:						
Wildlife:						
Vegetation:						

Caught: _____   Lost: _____

Substrate:

Observations:

TRIP NARRATIVE

SETTING   FISH LOG

Date:	Species	Size	Fly	Rig	Lie	Time
Duration: Begin:						
End:						
Stream:						
Location/Access:						
Weather:						
Temperature: Air:						
Water:						
Discharge/Stage:						
Companions:						
Wildlife:						
Vegetation:						

Caught: _____   Lost: _____

Substrate:

Observations:

TRIP NARRATIVE

SETTING

FISH LOG

Date:	Species	Size	Fly	Rig	Lie	Time
Duration: Begin: End:						
Stream:						
Location/Access:						
Weather:						
Temperature: Air: Water:						
Discharge/Stage:						
Companions:						
Wildlife:						
Vegetation:						

Caught: _____   Lost: _____

Substrate:

Observations:

TRIP NARRATIVE

SETTING

FISH LOG

Date:	Species	Size	Fly	Rig	Lie	Time
Duration: Begin:						
End:						
Stream:						
Location/Access:						
Weather:						
Temperature: Air:						
Water:						
Discharge/Stage:						
Companions:						
Wildlife:						
Vegetation:						

Caught: _____   Lost: _____

Substrate:

Observations:

TRIP NARRATIVE

SETTING

FISH LOG

Date:	Species	Size	Fly	Rig	Lie	Time
Duration: Begin:						
End:						
Stream:						
Location/Access:						
Weather:						
Temperature: Air:						
Water:						
Discharge/Stage:						
Companions:						
Wildlife:						
Vegetation:						

Caught: _____   Lost: _____

Substrate:

Observations:

TRIP NARRATIVE

F I S H   L O G

Date:	Species	Size	Fly	Rig	Lie	Time
Duration: Begin: End:						
Stream:						
Location/Access:						
Weather:						
Temperature: Air: Water:						
Discharge/Stage:						
Companions:						
Wildlife:						
Vegetation:						

Caught: _____   Lost: _____

Substrate:

Observations:

TRIP NARRATIVE

F I S H   L O G

Date:	Species	Size	Fly	Rig	Lie	Time
Duration: Begin: End:						
Stream:						
Location/Access:						
Weather:						
Temperature: Air: Water:						
Discharge/Stage:						
Companions:						
Wildlife:						
Vegetation:						

Caught: _____   Lost: _____

Substrate:

Observations:

TRIP NARRATIVE

SETTING

FISH LOG

Date:	Species	Size	Fly	Rig	Lie	Time
Duration: Begin: End:						
Stream:						
Location/Access:						
Weather:						
Temperature: Air: Water:						
Discharge/Stage:						
Companions:						
Wildlife:						
Vegetation:						

Caught: _____   Lost: _____

Substrate:

Observations:

TRIP NARRATIVE

SETTING

FISH LOG

Date:	Species	Size	Fly	Rig	Lie	Time
Duration: Begin: End:						
Stream:						
Location/Access:						
Weather:						
Temperature: Air: Water:						
Discharge/Stage:						
Companions:						
Wildlife:						
Vegetation:						

Caught: _____   Lost: _____

Substrate: Observations:

TRIP NARRATIVE

SETTING

FISH LOG

Date:	Species	Size	Fly	Rig	Lie	Time
Duration: Begin: End:						
Stream:						
Location/Access:						
Weather:						
Temperature: Air: Water:						
Discharge/Stage:						
Companions:						
Wildlife:						
Vegetation:						
	Caught: _____			Lost: _____		
Substrate:	Observations:					

TRIP NARRATIVE

SETTING   FISH LOG

Date:	Species	Size	Fly	Rig	Lie	Time
Duration: Begin:						
End:						
Stream:						
Location/Access:						
Weather:						
Temperature: Air:						
Water:						
Discharge/Stage:						
Companions:						
Wildlife:						
Vegetation:						

Caught: _____   Lost: _____

Substrate: Observations:

TRIP NARRATIVE

S E T T I N G F I S H L O G

Date:	Species	Size	Fly	Rig	Lie	Time
Duration: Begin: End:						
Stream:						
Location/Access:						
Weather:						
Temperature: Air: Water:						
Discharge/Stage:						
Companions:						
Wildlife:						
Vegetation:						

Caught: _____   Lost: _____

Substrate:

Observations:

TRIP NARRATIVE

FISH LOG

Date:	Species	Size	Fly	Rig	Lie	Time
Duration: Begin: End:						
Stream:						
Location/Access:						
Weather:						
Temperature: Air: Water:						
Discharge/Stage:						
Companions:						
Wildlife:						
Vegetation:						

Caught: _____   Lost: _____

Substrate: Observations:

TRIP NARRATIVE

SETTING

FISH LOG

Date:	Species	Size	Fly	Rig	Lie	Time
Duration: Begin: End:						
Stream:						
Location/Access:						
Weather:						
Temperature: Air: Water:						
Discharge/Stage:						
Companions:						
Wildlife:						
Vegetation:						

Caught: _____   Lost: _____

Substrate:

Observations:

TRIP NARRATIVE

SETTING

FISH LOG

Date:	Species	Size	Fly	Rig	Lie	Time
Duration: Begin: End:						
Stream:						
Location/Access:						
Weather:						
Temperature: Air: Water:						
Discharge/Stage:						
Companions:						
Wildlife:						
Vegetation:						

Caught: _____   **Lost:** _____

Substrate:

Observations:

TRIP NARRATIVE

SETTING

FISH LOG

Date:	Species	Size	Fly	Rig	Lie	Time
Duration: Begin: End:						
Stream:						
Location/Access:						
Weather:						
Temperature: Air: Water:						
Discharge/Stage:						
Companions:						
Wildlife:						
Vegetation:						

Caught: _____   Lost: _____

Substrate:

Observations:

TRIP NARRATIVE

FISH LOG

Date:	Species	Size	Fly	Rig	Lie	Time
Duration: Begin:						
End:						
Stream:						
Location/Access:						
Weather:						
Temperature: Air:						
Water:						
Discharge/Stage:						
Companions:						
Wildlife:						
Vegetation:						

Caught: _____   Lost: _____

Substrate:

Observations:

TRIP NARRATIVE

SETTING

FISH LOG

Date:	Species	Size	Fly	Rig	Lie	Time
Duration: Begin: End:						
Stream:						
Location/Access:						
Weather:						
Temperature: Air: Water:						
Discharge/Stage:						
Companions:						
Wildlife:						
Vegetation:						

Caught: _____   Lost: _____

Substrate:

Observations:

TRIP NARRATIVE

SETTING   FISH LOG

Date:	Species	Size	Fly	Rig	Lie	Time
Duration: Begin: End:						
Stream:						
Location/Access:						
Weather:						
Temperature: Air: Water:						
Discharge/Stage:						
Companions:						
Wildlife:						
Vegetation:						

Caught: _____   Lost: _____

Substrate: Observations:

TRIP NARRATIVE

SETTING

FISH LOG

Date:	Species	Size	Fly	Rig	Lie	Time
Duration: Begin:						
End:						
Stream:						
Location/Access:						
Weather:						
Temperature: Air:						
Water:						
Discharge/Stage:						
Companions:						
Wildlife:						
Vegetation:						

Caught: _____   Lost: _____

Substrate:

Observations:

TRIP NARRATIVE

SETTING

Date:	Species	Size	Fly	Rig	Lie	Time
Duration: Begin: End:						
Stream:						
Location/Access:						
Weather:						
Temperature: Air: Water:						
Discharge/Stage:						
Companions:						
Wildlife:						
Vegetation:						

Caught: _____   Lost: _____

Substrate:

Observations:

TRIP NARRATIVE

FISH LOG

Date:	Species	Size	Fly	Rig	Lie	Time
Duration: Begin:						
End:						
Stream:						
Location/Access:						
Weather:						
Temperature: Air:						
Water:						
Discharge/Stage:						
Companions:						
Wildlife:						
Vegetation:						

Caught: _____   Lost: _____

Substrate:

Observations:

TRIP NARRATIVE

SETTING   FISH LOG

Date:	Species	Size	Fly	Rig	Lie	Time
Duration: Begin: End:						
Stream:						
Location/Access:						
Weather:						
Temperature: Air: Water:						
Discharge/Stage:						
Companions:						
Wildlife:						
Vegetation:						

Caught: _____   Lost: _____

Substrate:

Observations:

TRIP NARRATIVE

SETTING   FISH LOG

Date:	Species	Size	Fly	Rig	Lie	Time
Duration: Begin: End:						
Stream:						
Location/Access:						
Weather:						
Temperature: Air: Water:						
Discharge/Stage:						
Companions:						
Wildlife:						
Vegetation:						

Caught: _____ Lost: _____

Substrate: Observations:

TRIP NARRATIVE

SETTING   FISH LOG

Date:	Species	Size	Fly	Rig	Lie	Time
Duration: Begin: End:						
Stream:						
Location/Access:						
Weather:						
Temperature: Air: Water:						
Discharge/Stage:						
Companions:						
Wildlife:						
Vegetation:						

Caught: _____   Lost: _____

Substrate: Observations:

SETTING   FISH LOG

Date:	Species	Size	Fly	Rig	Lie	Time
Duration: Begin: End:						
Stream:						
Location/Access:						
Weather:						
Temperature: Air: Water:						
Discharge/Stage:						
Companions:						
Wildlife:						
Vegetation:						

Caught: _____   **Lost:** _____

Substrate:

Observations:

TRIP NARRATIVE

SETTING

FISH LOG

	Species	Size	Fly	Rig	Lie	Time
Date:						
Duration: Begin: End:						
Stream:						
Location/Access:						
Weather:						
Temperature: Air: Water:						
Discharge/Stage:						
Companions:						
Wildlife:						
Vegetation:						

Caught: _____   Lost: _____

Substrate:

Observations:

TRIP NARRATIVE

Date:	Species	Size	Fly	Rig	Lie	Time
Duration: Begin: End:						
Stream:						
Location/Access:						
Weather:						
Temperature: Air: Water:						
Discharge/Stage:						
Companions:						
Wildlife:						
Vegetation:						

Caught: _____   Lost: _____

Substrate:

Observations:

TRIP NARRATIVE

SETTING

FISH LOG

	Species	Size	Fly	Rig	Lie	Time
Date:						
Duration: Begin: End:						
Stream:						
Location/Access:						
Weather:						
Temperature: Air: Water:						
Discharge/Stage:						
Companions:						
Wildlife:						
Vegetation:						

Caught: _____   Lost: _____

Substrate:

Observations:

TRIP NARRATIVE

SETTING

FISH LOG

Date:	Species	Size	Fly	Rig	Lie	Time
Duration: Begin: End:						
Stream:						
Location/Access:						
Weather:						
Temperature: Air: Water:						
Discharge/Stage:						
Companions:						
Wildlife:						
Vegetation:						
Substrate:	Caught: _____ Lost: _____ Observations:					

TRIP NARRATIVE

SETTING   FISH LOG

Date:	Species	Size	Fly	Rig	Lie	Time
Duration: Begin: End:						
Stream:						
Location/Access:						
Weather:						
Temperature: Air: Water:						
Discharge/Stage:						
Companions:						
Wildlife:						
Vegetation:						

Caught: _____   **Lost:** _____

Observations:

Substrate:

TRIP NARRATIVE

FISH LOG

Date:	Species	Size	Fly	Rig	Lie	Time
Duration: Begin: End:						
Stream:						
Location/Access:						
Weather:						
Temperature: Air: Water:						
Discharge/Stage:						
Companions:						
Wildlife:						
Vegetation:						

Caught: _____   Lost: _____

Substrate:

Observations:

TRIP NARRATIVE

SETTING

FISH LOG

Date:	Species	Size	Fly	Rig	Lie	Time
Duration: Begin: End:						
Stream:						
Location/Access:						
Weather:						
Temperature: Air: Water:						
Discharge/Stage:						
Companions:						
Wildlife:						
Vegetation:						

Caught: _____   Lost: _____

Substrate:

Observations:

TRIP NARRATIVE

SETTING

FISH LOG

Date:	Species	Size	Fly	Rig	Lie	Time
Duration: Begin:						
End:						
Stream:						
Location/Access:						
Weather:						
Temperature: Air:						
Water:						
Discharge/Stage:						
Companions:						
Wildlife:						
Vegetation:						

Caught: _____   Lost: _____

Substrate:

Observations:

TRIP NARRATIVE

SETTING   FISH LOG

Date:	Species	Size	Fly	Rig	Lie	Time
Duration: Begin: End:						
Stream:						
Location/Access:						
Weather:						
Temperature: Air: Water:						
Discharge/Stage:						
Companions:						
Wildlife:						
Vegetation:						

Caught: _____   **Lost:** _____

Substrate:

Observations:

TRIP NARRATIVE

SETTING

FISH LOG

Date:	Species	Size	Fly	Rig	Lie	Time
Duration: Begin: End:						
Stream:						
Location/Access:						
Weather:						
Temperature: Air: Water:						
Discharge/Stage:						
Companions:						
Wildlife:						
Vegetation:						

Caught: _____   Lost: _____

Substrate:

Observations:

TRIP NARRATIVE

SETTING			FISH LOG			
Date:	**Species**	**Size**	**Fly**	**Rig**	**Lie**	**Time**
Duration: Begin: End:						
Stream:						
Location/Access:						
Weather:						
Temperature: Air: Water:						
Discharge/Stage:						
Companions:						
Wildlife:						
Vegetation:						
	Caught: _____			Lost: _____		
Substrate:	Observations:					

TRIP NARRATIVE

FISH LOG

Date:	Species	Size	Fly	Rig	Lie	Time
Duration: Begin: End:						
Stream:						
Location/Access:						
Weather:						
Temperature: Air: Water:						
Discharge/Stage:						
Companions:						
Wildlife:						
Vegetation:						

Caught: _____   Lost: _____

Substrate:

Observations:

TRIP NARRATIVE

SETTING

FISH LOG

Date:	Species	Size	Fly	Rig	Lie	Time
Duration: Begin: End:						
Stream:						
Location/Access:						
Weather:						
Temperature: Air: Water:						
Discharge/Stage:						
Companions:						
Wildlife:						
Vegetation:						

Caught: _____   Lost: _____

Substrate:

Observations:

TRIP NARRATIVE

SETTING   FISH LOG

Date:	Species	Size	Fly	Rig	Lie	Time
Duration: Begin: End:						
Stream:						
Location/Access:						
Weather:						
Temperature: Air: Water:						
Discharge/Stage:						
Companions:						
Wildlife:						
Vegetation:						

Caught: _____   Lost: _____

Substrate: Observations:

TRIP NARRATIVE

Date:	Species	Size	Fly	Rig	Lie	Time
Duration: Begin: End:						
Stream:						
Location/Access:						
Weather:						
Temperature: Air: Water:						
Discharge/Stage:						
Companions:						
Wildlife:						
Vegetation:						

Caught: _____ Lost: _____

Substrate: Observations:

TRIP NARRATIVE

SETTING

FISH LOG

Date:	Species	Size	Fly	Rig	Lie	Time
Duration: Begin: End:						
Stream:						
Location/Access:						
Weather:						
Temperature: Air: Water:						
Discharge/Stage:						
Companions:						
Wildlife:						
Vegetation:						

Caught: _____   Lost: _____

Substrate:

Observations:

TRIP NARRATIVE

SETTING

FISH LOG

Date:	Species	Size	Fly	Rig	Lie	Time
Duration: Begin:						
End:						
Stream:						
Location/Access:						
Weather:						
Temperature: Air:						
Water:						
Discharge/Stage:						
Companions:						
Wildlife:						
Vegetation:						

Caught: _____   Lost: _____

Substrate:

Observations:

TRIP NARRATIVE

SETTING

FISH LOG

Date:	Species	Size	Fly	Rig	Lie	Time
Duration: Begin: End:						
Stream:						
Location/Access:						
Weather:						
Temperature: Air: Water:						
Discharge/Stage:						
Companions:						
Wildlife:						
Vegetation:						

Caught: _____   Lost: _____

Substrate: Observations:

TRIP NARRATIVE

FISH LOG

Date:	Species	Size	Fly	Rig	Lie	Time
Duration: Begin:						
End:						
Stream:						
Location/Access:						
Weather:						
Temperature: Air:						
Water:						
Discharge/Stage:						
Companions:						
Wildlife:						
Vegetation:						

Caught: _____   Lost: _____

Substrate:

Observations:

TRIP NARRATIVE

SETTING   FISH LOG

Date:	Species	Size	Fly	Rig	Lie	Time
Duration: Begin: End:						
Stream:						
Location/Access:						
Weather:						
Temperature: Air: Water:						
Discharge/Stage:						
Companions:						
Wildlife:						
Vegetation:						

Caught: _____ Lost: _____

Substrate:

Observations:

TRIP NARRATIVE

Date:	Species	Size	Fly	Rig	Lie	Time
Duration: Begin: End:						
Stream:						
Location/Access:						
Weather:						
Temperature: Air: Water:						
Discharge/Stage:						
Companions:						
Wildlife:						
Vegetation:						
	Caught: _____ Lost: _____					
Substrate:	Observations:					

TRIP NARRATIVE

SETTING

FISH LOG

Date:	Species	Size	Fly	Rig	Lie	Time
Duration: Begin: End:						
Stream:						
Location/Access:						
Weather:						
Temperature: Air: Water:						
Discharge/Stage:						
Companions:						
Wildlife:						
Vegetation:						

Caught: _____ **Lost:** _____

Substrate:

Observations:

TRIP NARRATIVE

SETTING   FISH LOG

Date:	Species	Size	Fly	Rig	Lie	Time
Duration: Begin: End:						
Stream:						
Location/Access:						
Weather:						
Temperature: Air: Water:						
Discharge/Stage:						
Companions:						
Wildlife:						
Vegetation:						
Substrate:	Caught: _____ Lost: _____ Observations:					

TRIP NARRATIVE

FISH LOG

Date:	Species	Size	Fly	Rig	Lie	Time
Duration: Begin: End:						
Stream:						
Location/Access:						
Weather:						
Temperature: Air: Water:						
Discharge/Stage:						
Companions:						
Wildlife:						
Vegetation:						

Caught: _____   **Lost:** _____

Substrate:

Observations:

TRIP NARRATIVE

www.ingramcontent.com/pod-product-compliance
Lightning Source LLC
Chambersburg PA
CBHW041935260326
41914CB00010B/1300